The Timetraveller's Guide to...

TUDOR LONDON

First published in 2004 by Watling St Publishing
The Glen
Southrop
Lechlade
Gloucestershire
GL7 3NY

Printed in Italy

ISBN 1-904153-09-7

24681097531

Design: Mackerel Limited
Illustrations: Mark Davis

www.tempus-publishing.com

The Timetraveller's Guide to...

TUDOR LONDON

Natasha Narayan

WATLING STREET

Natasha Narayan tried her hand at everything from waitressing to apple picking with equal lack of success before she found a small niche in journalism. Her pieces appeared in papers including the *Guardian*, the *Observer* and the *Daily Mail* and she worked as a foreign correspondent in Bosnia, Albania and Georgia. She was also an education correspondent on the *Observer* and, briefly, a presenter on the world's worst satellite breakfast show. She lives in North London with her family.

For my grandmother Saraswati.

Contents

INTRODUCTION

This is a guide to Tudor London. But be warned: it is not one of those guidebooks that tells you where to find the pretty buildings and nice galleries. This is really, really rough.

In this book you'll have to hold your nose as you venture through stinking streets and teeming alleys. You'll behold disgusting beheadings and terrible tortures. You'll smell rotten food and putrid diseases.

If you were forty-five in Tudor London you were probably toothless, wrinkly and doddering. This was a time when the smell of excrement was as familiar to Londoners as petrol fumes are today. When people's teeth turned black and rotten from eating rich food. When doctors killed more people than they cured. Vicious diseases like the plague could wipe out half the people in your street. And if that didn't get you King Henry VIII, the mad Tudor axeman, might.

Lousy laws could see you getting your ear chopped off for stealing a loaf of bread. London was a sick place to live. Foul pits served as public toilets. Private toilets might just be a pile of rushes in the corner of your room or a chamber pot that could be tipped on a passerby in the alley below. The water was too disgusting to drink. Fresh water had to be bought from wandering water sellers, who collected it from fountains such as the Conduit in Cheapside. All in all being a Tudor Londoner was no picnic!

So clunk click, seatbelts on, for a ride back to stinkier, nastier times.

CHAPTER ONE

𝕬 𝕭𝖆𝖈𝖔𝖓'𝖘 𝕲𝖚𝖎𝖉𝖊 𝖙𝖔 𝕾𝖎𝖓 𝕮𝖎𝖙𝖞

London in the 1500s was a wicked town. A place that young 'bacons', or country boys, were warned against by their mums and dads. The Tudor capital was rough, tough, mean and most decidedly unclean.

Imagine you're a bacon, trudging into the city from the green pastures of Islington. First you come to the houses around Clerkenwell priory, where the monks live, then to the fields of Smithfield, where later on in the bloody century hundreds of people were burned for their faith.

You pass through the big gates of Newgate into the narrow festering lanes of the walled City of London itself. The stink is overpowering. Sewage and garbage mixed with perfumes like musk and ambergris, which the rich use to keep the smell at nose distance. The noise of carts and horses and hundreds of people calling out their wares. The crush of bodies sending you flying into the slimy, foul gutters if you're not careful. Is that a turnip you're stepping on or a bit of pig's bladder?

People are packed inside these medieval walls like sardines in a tin full of rubbish and sewage. Houses are built with one storey jutting out over the other – so they almost bang into each other in the centre of the narrow lanes. Very little sunlight and fresh air manage to sneak into the foul streets below. At sunset the city's gates clang shut and a watchman goes out to patrol the streets with his dog, his staff and his lantern, crying out to honest citizens to beware of fires and robbers:

Remember the clocks
Look well to your locks
Your fire and your light
And god give you good night

Five Stinking London Jobs

Match the yucky London job with the even more loathsome description

1) RAKER
2) CLAPPERDUDGEON
3) COUNTERFEIT CRANK
4) YEOMAN OF THE STOOL
5) SALTPETRE MAN
6) DUMMERER

A) A man who comes and collects your poo to turn into gunpowder

B) A beggar who sits in the filth and tries to get your sympathy by pretending to be deaf and dumb

C) A pretend beggar who creates his own sores and then sprinkles them with fresh cow's blood, salt and ratsbane to make them look more nasty

D) A beggar who pretends to have fits. He may eat soap to make himself foam at the mouth

E) A man who is paid to take away the nastiest slops from the sewers in a wheelbarrow

F) A man who helps King Henry VIII use his chamber pot.

Answers: 1E 2C 3D 4F 5A 6B

11

Seventy years later, in about 1570, in the reign of Queen Elizabeth, if you came into the city from the forests of Kent you came first to the suburb of Southwark. This seamy place was largely owned by the Bishop of Winchester but it seethed with conmen and criminals, with bear pits and theatres. It was home to the grim Marshalsea and Clink prisons as well as the grand houses of the toffs and was called the 'liberties' because the watchmen from the City of London didn't have power here.

It is easy to get across the river from Southwark. The Thames rings with cries of Eastward Ho! and Westward Ho! For a penny a boatman will row you across. Or you can walk across London Bridge – one of the city's wonders. This huge stone bridge is sagging with the fabulous houses of wealthy merchants.

The bloody heads of executed men decorate the poles of London Bridge's gatehouse. It is a stark warning to bacons – what might happen if you get into bad ways in sin city. Then you come to the fancy new royal palace of St James's. And then onwards to where the monks of Westminster Abbey, once the richest in England, lived (that was before Henry VIII closed down the abbeys and sacked all the monks).

The river is where the powerful pow-wow. On the river is the splendid palace of Whitehall, once the chief home of Henry VIII and all three of his children, Edward, Mary and Elizabeth.

Half a mile south of Whitehall is Westminster Hall and Westminster Abbey. All the most important stuff that decides the fate of poor little bacons like you goes on around here; kings address parliament in the Hall and worship in the Abbey. But it isn't London's bigness and grandness that makes your mum and dad warn you never to go there. It is the lowlifes: the toothless beggars who gape at you from on top of piles of rubbish as they pick at their own sores. The cutpurses who would rob you as soon as say hello. And the swindlers who go looking for innocents from the country to befriend and, well, swindle. No wonder you need a good guidebook to survive!

Especially if you are travelling back from the very unwhiffy 21st century.

The Really Rough Guide to
Tudor London

Copyright Watling Street Press 1599. By I B Whiffy.

Top tips for time travellers to help them survive their stay in the world's smelliest and toughest city! All the taverns and ordinaries (cheap food stalls) in these guides have been visited by our inspectors, who do not get free food or drinks and pay for their own meals. Some have come out alive. We have checked the sights out personally. Our star system is as follows.

* Too smelly and dirty for words. Stay Clear.
** Too, too smelly and dirty for words. Worth a visit.
*** Too, too, too smelly and dirty for words. Full marks!

Getting to London

Many visitors to London will enter it by boat. The boatmen are notorious cheats. Pay no more than a penny for this ride. And make sure you agree where you are to be set down. Many boatmen will take their passengers on rides across the Thames and you may end up many leagues from Westminster!

Sights

There are many fine sights in London. Most visitors will start with a tour of the grand palaces of Whitehall and Westminster before being taken along Strand east towards St Paul's Cathedral and the Royal Exchange. But for us there is only one sight that gets top marks for foul doings and gruesome tortures. Yes, the Tower of London***!

Here on Tower Green Henry VIII's second queen, Anne Boleyn, was beheaded. She is buried in the Chapel of St Peter Ad Vincula. Her alleged lovers lost their heads (in more senses than one) on Tower Hill. There have been sightings of Anne Boleyn's ghost at the Tower – so maybe she really was a witch as her disloyal husband claimed. The young Elizabeth was kept prisoner here by her half-sister Queen Mary, accused of helping the rebel Sir Thomas Wyatt. She came by boat into London's grimmest castle believing she would die and was locked up in the Bell Tower. (As you know she was later released and went on to become Queen.)

Queen Elizabeth imprisoned plenty of traitors and Catholics, plotters and innocent men here. Among them was Liz's onetime favourite, the Earl of Essex. Shakespeare's patron, the Earl of Southampton, was also imprisoned here. The foulest tortures were carried out in the Tower's gloomy dungeons (See the extract from The Torturer's Handbook later for more details.)

Accommodation

London is full of inns and taverns where you can get a bed for the night. But be warned – some of them may actually be fairly clean. Many taverns will supply you with a new-fangled mattress and pillows instead of the traditional log and straw. Rooms may have their own fires and there will be several travellers, except in the most expensive inns, sharing a room.

Eating

You never have to go hungry in London, provided you have a penny or six to spare. Ordinaries line the street in Bread Street and East Cheap. Boys run among the customers who sit at long wooden tables in a large room strewn with straw. The staw reeks of spit, vomit, dung, sewage and rotting food. You name it the rushes are mixed with it. Some ordinaries change their rushes every year. (These are the clean ones.)

The customers eat with their hands from the common trenchers (pieces of bread that you use as plates). The boys call out 'What do you lack?' and bring roasts, cuts of meat, chickens and pastries. There is plenty of noise and muck. Don't share a trencher with a diner who has the plague or the sweat. Sometimes these ordinaries are too clean for our liking**.

Tudor Fast Food

Some of the best food in London is sold hot on the streets.

In the bustling booksellers' markets around St Paul's Cathedral you can get lark and pigeon pies, pasties, nuts, sweetmeats and other fancies. (And there is a juicy smell of rotting corpse here too.) The Gingerbread Husbands on sale at the market in Cheapside are fantastic***.

Taverns

The George Inn, Southwark**

This is a very well known tavern which is built around a large and pleasant courtyard. Some jolly plays have been staged in the courtyard, patrons can enjoy the action from the large balconies.

Nowadays of course this pub can't really compete with the splendid Rose and the Globe Theatres. The clientele however is a mixed bunch and includes merchants and market men as well as many actors from the nearby theatres. Unsavoury writers like Will Shakespeare have been known to sup ale here. The ale is good, as is the claret. Food is reasonably priced. The herring pie and roast capons are recommended. The George is too clean to get our top star ranking! (The George can still be visited at 77 Borough High Street, Southwark. It was burnt down in the 1600s and rebuilt, but is still very like the Tudor inn.)

The White Hart, Southwark***

A very seedy inn with excellent cheap ale for a penny a flagon and a great crowd. Brews served here include: Huffe Cup, Mad Dog, Angel's Food, Lift Leg and Stride Wide. This place is dirty, stinky and seethes with lowlifes. Beware, cutpurses love the White Hart. If you consume too much of the ale don't trust anyone says you're their best friend. He may be a swindler. We love the White Hart. Top marks.

The Mitre***.

On the corner of Friday Street and Bread Street, Cheapside. Visit this pub for its fantastic minced pies. It is also very smelly, dirty and crowded with apprentices from the nearby market. You will be served by George. But be wary, George and his customers don't like strangers. Shakespeare's friend, the playwright Ben Jonson, writes, 'If any stranger comes in amongst 'em they all stand up and stare at him, as if he were some unknown beast.'

18

Shopping

Sir Thomas Gresham's Royal Exchange was opened by our Glorious Majesty Queen Elizabeth in 1571. What a splendid place with its broad avenues and columns. A marvel, an indoor super market! As everyone knows this has the biggest and best shops in the world. You can buy wigs, ruffs, embroideries and clothes and almost anything you desire here. This is for gentlemen of quality (and not for the likes of you). For secondhand clothes go to Birchin Lane.

For cloth and hats go to West Cheap and London Bridge Fishmongers are in Knight-riders Street (Knight Rider Street) and Bridge Street.

Wine and beer sellers near the river Thames and in Vintree (that's the Vintry in modern spelling).

For grocers go to Bucklesberrie (Bucklersbury).

For skinners go to Budge Row and Walbrooke (Walbrook).

The market at Cheapside has everything.

If you lose this guide don't worry. Many street names will help. Bread Street for example is next to Goldsmiths Row.

Smelliest Street

Stinking Lane*. Near St Nicholas Shambles and Fowle Alley
These narrow smelly streets thread through the heart of the city
of London. Beware of chamberpots emptied on your head. Of

offal in the gutters. Of the smell of mud,
dung, tobacco, sweaty toes, dirty shoes,
poo and stinking breath. Other very
smelly streets are Butchers' Lane, full of
offal and rotting meat and Stocks Market
where stall holders throw out rotting
vegetables.

Entertainment
Southwark***

The most dangerous place in
London. Watch out for
cutpurses and foists. This is
their natural habitat. Actors
are also known vagabonds and
may put on a play only to lure
you to part with your money.

Southwark has the noisiest,
bloodiest and best
entertainment in the whole
civilized world. Visit the Bear
Gardens at Bankside, by the
Thames for bear-baiting. For
theatres try out the Rose and
the Swan.

CHAPTER TWO

Top Tudor Twits

(or Kings and Queens to You)

The Tudor kings and queens were a pretty mean gang –
certainly bad people to get on the wrong side of. They'd chop
off your head sooner than they'd shake your hand. But they
weren't all bad for London. Under their rule the city exploded.
It went from a town of less than 50,000 people to a city three or
four times the size.

New four-storey houses rose on the ashes of humble market
stalls. Grand palaces, theatres, bear-baiting rings, even the
earliest supermarkets sprang up. Tudor London became the

vital, beating heart of an empire – as Queen Elizabeth's sailors staked their claims to bits of the new world such as the Americas.

London may have been prosperous but it was getting more jam-packed with people and houses every day. You just had to stroll down Butchers' Alley right by St Nicholas Shambles and Stinking Lane to see why the streets got their whiffy names.

While ordinary Londoners lived huddled together in a crumbling and stinky city the kings lorded it over them in their fantastic palaces. Elizabeth, for example, when she became Queen inherited more than two dozen palaces. The biggest was Whitehall Palace on the banks of the Thames, said to be the largest and ugliest in Europe. It was so sprawling it was more like a village than a castle. Then there was Hampton Court, also on the Thames, where 'Royal Tennis' was played. And the queen's favourite, Richmond Palace. Beyond this was Windsor Castle, in the country, not to mention Greenwich Palace, where she was born.

Here are some rhymes to help you remember which Tudor is which:

WANTED

FOR CRIMES AGAINST JUSTICE, HUMANITY AND COMMON SENSE

THE TUDORS

King of Clubs (King Henry VIII)

(1509–1547 – Wanted for being a serial killer, serial marrier, for too many hangings, beheadings and murders to list)

King Henry, most wanted of men
Ditched his first wife for young Anne Boleyn
When she gave birth to Liz
He got in a tiz
And killed her and married again

Nine of Clubs (King Edward VI)

(1547–1553 – Wanted for being a sickly nine-year-old when he came to the throne. Carried on Daddy's work and forced the Protestant faith on his people.)

Poor Eddie was crowned King at nine,
Too little to stomach much wine,
He was pale and quite sickly
And very often prickly
And Catholics thought him a swine

Queen of Diamonds
(Queen 'Bloody' Mary)
(1553–1558 – Wanted for the burnings of many
hundreds of Protestant martyrs)

Bloody Mary was quite another matter
She deepfried the Prots into batter.
Husband Philip of Spain
Was heard to complain,
'The old trout's as mad as a hatter.'

Queen of Hearts (Queen Elizabeth I)
(1558–1603 – Wanted for ordering the
execution of her cousin Mary, Queen of Scots
on fabricated evidence. Also wanted for the
execution of many Catholics and traitors. Some
of them innocent!)

Unlike her gargantuan dad
Queen Bess was as slim as a lad.
'I'm married to Blighty'
She told suitors in her nightie.
'So I'm afraid the answer's TOO BAD!'

(Founder of the dynasty King Henry VII is not being sought by the police –
detectives last night described him as being too normal to bother with!)

Anyone seeing suspects matching the descriptions of the above and acting
suspiciously should report to the city constables. BE WARNED: DO NOT
ATTEMPT AN ARREST YOURSELF – THE SUSPECTS ARE ARMED AND
DANGEROUS!

Tudor kings and queens could be foul to friends and foe alike – not to mention ordinary Londoners.

Admittedly, Henry VII, the one who started the dynasty by killing Richard III at the Battle of Boswell. wasn't that bad. He loved his wife, Elizabeth of York and his reign was pretty peaceful. He didn't make war abroad or go around killing people at home. The worst thing people said about him was that he was stingy. In fact his son executed more people in the first few years of his reign than old Dad did in his whole life. And oh boy, what a son. A monster in human form.

Henry VIII has a fair claim to being the biggest, baddest monarch in London's history. He certainly was the biggest. The thing is, when big Henry got the king job in 1509 he looked like he was going to be great news for Londoners. He was clever and witty as well as a bit of a heartthrob. Young Henry Tudor was six foot two inches of prime royal beefcake, ace at jousting and horse-riding and with a luuverly, swoony voice when he sang *Greensleeves* (his number-one hit) to the ladies.

When he died in 1547 he was a right old fatty, who suffered from gout (a disease of overeating), sore legs (would you like to have to carry around all that fat?) and constipation (less said here the better, I think). We know from his armour in the Tower of London that his waist measured 54 inches. Horrible Henry's rule was a reign of terror. Just to get a son to continue his line he divorced his wife Katherine of Aragon and split with the Pope, who was dead against it. Then he declared he was the English Pope and founded a new Church, the Church of England. He also beheaded loads of nobles and priests as well as two of his six wives and divorced two other wives.

According to the Tudor historian Raphael Holinshed, whose Chronicles of England were published in 1578, 72,000 thieves and vagabonds were hanged in Henry VIII's reign. That is two and a half per cent of England's three million subjects – as a percentage, Henry killed almost as many people as modern monsters Hitler and Stalin!

But if he was mean with other people, he never stinted on his own meat and drink and pleasures. Lolling about at his sumptuous palace in Whitehall by the Thames he indulged in days of feasting, jousting and entertainment. His subjects might have been abject (pretty sad) but Henry had a great time...

Henry VIII Seven-Step Diet Plan

Step One

Don't be a peasant or a pleb.
Poor people eat horse food:
beans, oats, barley, lentils. For
treats they get raw turnips,
sheep's feet and even weeds
like dandelion and sorrel. They
can get hungry and starve,
which is very bad manners.

Step Two

Always have at least ten courses at a meal. Here is a sample of
the menu I recommended for my bastard son, the Duke of
Richmond, when he was six:

First course: soup with two rounds of brawn, a helping of beef
or mutton, with either swan or goose, 3 roast capons 28 pounds
of roast meat and biscuit. Second course: more soup, 4 roast
rabbits, 14 pigeons, 4 partridges, a wildfowl, fruit and biscuits
along with 4 gallons of ale and 2 pitchers of wine. (Of course
even my son can't eat all this grub. I s'pose he can give the
leftovers to the poor. But if he keeps on trying he'll soon fatten
up nicely.)

Step Three

Be carried about by a team of underlings on a chair. This is useful when you want to watch my favourite sports of hunting or hawking. The underlings can wrap you up against the cold and seat you on a horse. (Make sure you get a good, strong mount, a weak horse might collapse under the strain.)

Step Four

Have a special system of pulleys and ropes built to hoist you around at your castles – saves on the tedious business of actually climbing the stairs.

Step Five

Have plenty of wives. If you get sick of one you can always chop off her head. Or if she is a foreign princess like my first wife Katherine of Aragon or my fourth wife Anne of Cleves, divorce her. And don't limit yourself to wives, make sure you have plenty of wenches for mistresses. They all get nervous and none of them dare nag you about eating too much.

Step Six

Order plenty of executions. Executions are exciting and keep the appetite whetted even when you're enormously fat. In my time I've executed people like Sir Thomas More, advisors like Thomas Cromwell, zealous Protestants like Anne Askew, Catholics like Bishop Fisher, nobles like the Countess of Salisbury and loads of common people. You name it, I've executed it! If you want to make the executions extra exciting get them for high treason. My laws made it high treason to prophesy the time of my death or deny any of my titles (like my being the head of the Church of England, which lots of Catholics denied). Those guilty were cut down from hanging while still alive and then had their privates cut off and were disembowelled while still alive. The bowels were then burnt before their eyes. Finally they were beheaded and cut into quarters. That's my idea of Good Clean Fun!

Step Seven

Make sure you get to be king. Being king is pure jam!

The single most important obsession of Henry's life was to have a son. And Jane Seymour, his third wife, was lucky, she gave him one. She was also lucky in that she died before Henry had time to get sick of her and chop her head off. When Henry died his nine-year-old son Edward succeeded him as king.

Edward was a frail, thin, clever lad. While other lads his age played with sticks and whistles Edward studied and studied and studied. He knew Latin and history, the names of all the ports in France and the good winds and tides for sailing to them – because a king must know these things. His favourite subject was GOD. He was a Protestant with a vengeance. There was nothing he liked better than to sit, his notebook and pen to hand, while the preacher droned on for several hours. But though he was the king of England, Edward was still a kid.

A succession of nobles and uncles ruled and schemed in his name. He was often in danger from kidnap plots because the person who had the king in his charge would become the power behind the throne. But Ed was a Tudor and he thought there were spies and plotters everywhere. He was determined not to be taken advantage of. He even wrote his diary in Greek letters so his attendants would not be able to read it.

When his uncle Lord Somerset, the Lord Protector talked to him, he always knelt (which must have been tough on his knees). But when Edward was very naughty he had to be told off. No tutor, not even Archbishop Cranmer, dared whip the King for being naughty so the whipping boy was invented. A whipping boy was someone the King was fond of who could be whipped when Edward was naughty. Ed's whipping boy was his best friend Barnaby Fitzpatrick – the son of an Irish chief who had been sent to the English court as a hostage for his dad's loyalty. Barnaby must have thought 'With friends like that, who needs enemies?'

Edward and His Whipping Boy

(*We are in Edward's lavish bedchamber in his chief royal residence on the river Thames at Whitehall. Edward is lying in bed reading the scriptures — his favourite hobby. Enter Archbishop Cranmer, very grand in his red and gold robes and following behind him, two hefty gentlemen of the chamber carrying a huge, steaming bucket of hot water.*)

Cranmer: (*kneeling before the king*) Majesty, it is time for your bath.

Edward: (*not bothering to look up from his book*) Begone, thou currish clay-brained codpiece.

Cranmer: Sire, I must press you.

Edward: Had one last year.

Cranmer: There has been noticed a most malodorous smell about your person. All the musk in China cannot conceal this putrid offence for much longer. We have important business afoot. We must think of your betrothal to your baby cousin, Mary, Queen of Scots.

Edward: Hate baths. I won't, I won't, I won't. Anyway, don't want to get married. Marriage is silly.
(*Edward sticks out his tongue at the archbishop and goes back to his Bible*).

Cranmer: (*sighing*) You leave me no choice, Sire.
(*He calls for an attendant who gives him a whip. Another attendant brings forth Barnaby Fitzpatrick.*)

Cranmer: Take off your shirt, boy.
(*Barnaby takes off his shirt silently and proudly, though his*

lips tremble, while Edward swears loudly. Cranmer whips Fitzpatrick. THWACK *goes the whip. Cranmer looks cross and red, like he'd really like to be whipping the young king. Edward shouts to Cranmer to stop but he takes no notice. Fitzpatrick's back, which is covered with sores, is now running with blood. By now Ed has had enough. He runs to the attendant who guards his bedchamber, snatches his sword and advances towards Cranmer, who backs away in panic. But instead of attacking Cranmer Edward lays the sword on Barnaby's shoulder and slowly, ceremonially, knights him.)*

Edward: Arise, Sir Barnaby Fitzpatrick. None of the gentlemen knighted by my father King Henry VIII has shed so much blood for their sovereign as you have for me. (*He drops his sword and hugs Barnaby.*) Besides, you're my only true friend in this horrid place. (*Glaring at Cranmer*) All right, you old crosspatch. YOU WIN! (*He plunges into the hot water.*)

When Edward died, at the age of fifteen, some people breathed a sigh of relief. His sister Mary may have been a woman, but at least she was a grown-up. Mary was just as religious as Edward but while he was a raving Protestant, she was a raving Catholic.

Pity the poor Tudor people. They can't have known what day it was – faithwise – with their yo-yo rulers. The Pope rules under Henry, then he sucks. The pope sucks under Ed. The Pope rules under Mary. The Pope sucks again under Liz! No wonder that some of Bloody Mary's victims were just plain confused!

She just couldn't wait to get started bullying all the Protestants who had sprung up everywhere. She thought they were just so much human litter that needed to be cleaned away.

In 1554 she married the Catholic King Philip of Spain. She hoped that this powerful alliance would cement England as a Catholic country. Handily, she was also madly in love with King Phil and hoped desperately to give him a son. But she was as unlucky as her mum, Katherine of Aragon. King Phil on the other hand was a bit bored with Queen Mary and thought her a bit plain and a bit pious. He soon left England and spent his time making merry abroad. With Phil away Queen Mary got on with the business of roasting Protestants, though Phil warned her to be careful. He was afraid that already unpopular Spaniards would be blamed. At least 280 Protestants were burned by Mary. Many of them were burned at the stake in Smithfield in East London. (Smithfield is now a meat market. Puts you off your next beefburger, doesn't it.)

The Underground Protestant News

By your special reporter John Foxe, who has risked life and limb to bring you this newsflash from Smithfield,

4 February

A bitterly cold day, as if the Lord weeps tears of ice for his martyr, John Rogers. For truly Mister Rogers is a Son of God and preacher of his word.

He is condemned to burn by those around Queen Mary for spreading the true Protestant word. Rogers has rotted in a foul cell in Newgate Prison for a year, his wife and eleven children cruelly denied the right to visit him.

This morning the Sheriff, Mr Woodruff, showed Rogers a letter promising him freedom if he recanted. But firm and proud Rogers sayeth: 'That which I have preached with my lips I will seal with my blood'.

So he was taken to Smithfield to burn. The torches at the stalls of sellers of pasties and cakes were put out by the Queen's men. But people brought

candles. A murmuring, angry crowd gathered as Rogers walked in chains from Newgate past his own church of St Sepulchre in Holborn to the fields at Smithfield.

At Smithfield he was chained to the stake, on top of a pile of faggots. His wife and children watched silently as the flames licked the wood and then burnt their way upwards. Strong to the end Rogers prayed, holding his hands together as if washing them in the flames. Thus was a true English martyr born.

By her cruel burnings Bloody Mary did more than Henry and Edward to make the people of London turn to the Protestant faith. When she died in 1558, after just five years on the throne, not many tears were shed for her in London's streets and alleys.

Next up was Mary's half-sister, Queen Elizabeth. Now Liz was a Tudor and so consequently had a cruel streak. But she was also brilliant, strong, proud and able to take counsel wisely. In fact, she was much more of a king than either her dad or her half brother.

In her subjects 'Good Queen Bess' – as they nicknamed her – inspired slavish love and loyalty. This was partly because she cleverly lost no opportunity to tell them how much she loved them.

Tudor Sunday Times

Free Coronation Supplement   15 January 1559

Thousands Flock To See
New Queen

By Royal Reporter Penny Slavish

Crowds lined the streets today to witness the historic coronation of Queen Elizabeth I. Shoulder to shoulder stood costermongers and knights, nobles and peasants, all thrilling with awe at the sight of her majesty's most beautiful and heavenly figure.

Dressed in gold robes, a gold mantle and an ermine cape, Elizabeth appeared before us. Her hair is of a most celestial gold and her face as pale as the moon. Her eyes do glow most wonderfully. She appeared more like goddess than queen but though exalted in rank she had a kind word for even the most humble and did frequently tell us how much she loved us. We love her back.

Three miles did the Queen journey in a chariot draped with crimson velvet. In Cheapside a child shouted, 'Remember old King Harry the Eighth' and the Queen's smile was most brilliant. An old lady thrust some rosemary in the royal chariot, which was still there when our Queen arrived at Westminster Abbey at dusk.

At the Abbey our Queen walked down a purple carpet, to the music of drummers and pipe players. After she departed into the abbey, the crowd fell on the carpet and wrenched pieces from where her blessed feet had stepped.

Our young Queen has impressed everyone with her wisdom and maturity. Her enemies are plotting but she remains defiant. There have been reports of vile popish plots against Elizabeth. Wax figures of the queen have been found, pierced through the heart with needles. Foreigners have not hesitated to invoke the devil against her.

But the omens are good. Royal magician Dr John Dee has prophesied that Elizabeth's reign will be a long and golden one of peace and prosperity.

Elizabeth will heal the bloody rifts that have divided brother from brother, between Protestant and Catholic, and lead our nation to greatness. May this reporter take the opportunity to assure Queen Elizabeth of her everlasting love and devotion.

So Queen Liz was quite something. Arguably she was the greatest monarch in our history. Under her reign writers like William Shakespeare and Christopher Marlowe flourished, grand houses were built and licensed pirates like Sir Walter Raleigh and Francis Drake explored the world, claiming bits of other people's countries as their own. But crime also flourished. In fact it became just as much of an art form as Shakespeare's plays…

CHAPTER THREE

The London Underworld

Honest Tudor countrymen were terrified that their kids would want to go to London. As we know, the city was notorious …

In small villages people kept tabs on each other and wrongdoers were punished. But it was easy to get lost in the big city. Lurking under the seemingly honest façade of taverns and eating houses was a seamy underworld. The criminal underground was smarter and better organized than the forces of law and order. So criminals grew fat and rich.

A Bacon's Guide to

If you wanted to survive in Tudor London you need to keep your wits about you. Here's a quiz to see how alley smart you are:

1) *You are in a trendy bowling alley, mixing with actors, writers, blacksmiths and costermongers (dodgy street sellers). You're pretty hot at bowling and when someone invites you to bet on a game, do you?*

A) *Take them up on their wager. You were champion at bowling on the village green*

B) *Bow out. Your mum warned you never to gamble.*

C) *Be very wary. The floors of bowling alleys are often made slippery with water or oil so that only the cheat knows how to win.*

2) *You're taking a stroll down Paul's Walk, the huge central aisle of St Paul's Cathedral when a well-dressed man falls in a faint in front of you. Do you?*

A) *Rush to assist him – you never know, you might get a reward.*

B) *Rush to assist him, you're in a cathedral, how dangerous can it be?*

C) *Stay well clear. He might be a cutpurse, who'll steal your money as you try and help him.*

Big City Low Life

3) At a gambling den, a man invites you to join him in cheating a third player. He promises huge profits. Would you?

A) Say yes, it's wrong but you need the money to survive in London.

B) Say no, strangers never win in London dens.

C) Say yes, the swindler has shown you the rigged card deck.

4) You're taking in a play at the theatre when you are suddenly hailed by a man you don't recognize, who claims to have known you as a young boy. The man knows your name, your business and claims to know your parents. He advises you not to wear your gold ring where it can be easily stolen, but to hide it inside your gown. Do you?

A) Not trust him, he could have got your name and information about you from your servant. But it was good advice so hide the ring.

B) Not trust him, so ignore his advice.

C) Trust him. You've got a really bad memory.

Answers: 1C 2C 3B 4B
Can you spot a common strand? Yep, that's right. Never trust anyone, however friendly, in Tudor London!

A Beggar's Opera

If you've done well in the quiz above you might fancy you're a pretty smart Tudor aleck. But you need to be more than suspicious to survive in London. How much of the underworld lingo – or peddlar's cant – could you figure out?

1) Was a *curber?*

A) A pavement on which beggars sat?
B) An instrument for cutting your fingers off?
C) An angler, who used a hook to steal clothes from open windows

2) Was a *gybe?*

A) A horrible insult
B) A fake document
C) A curse against the king punishable by death

3) Was a *cuttle bung?*

A) A type of meat that was marinated in urine?
B) A game, a bit like Scrabble which King Henry VIII invented
C) A knife which cutpurses used to nip and cut the purses of unsuspecting innocents

4) Were *hearing cheats?*

A) Ears
B) Men who swore false statements in a court of law
C) Pigs

5) Was a *cony?*

A) A rabbit
B) A simpleton who was swindled by a cony-catcher?
C) One of the new-fangled policemen

6) Was a *prigger of prancers?*

A) A dancing beggar
B) A horse thief
C) A bicycle?

7) Was a *horn thumb*?

A) A beggar
B) A sliver of horn attached to the thumb for cutting purses
C) A disease suffered by criminals who had their thumbs cut off

8) Was a *padder*?

A) A palace
B) A house of thieves
C) A highway robber

9) Did *stalled to the rogue* mean?

A) Being tricked out of your money?
B) Becoming a member of a beggars' club
C) Being drunk

10) Was a *swigman*?

A) A peddlar
B) A conman
C) A drunkard

11) Was a *wild dell*?

A) A wild place in the city
B) A thieves' house
C) A female tramp

12) Was *figging law*?

A) The cutpurse's art
B) The unjust laws of Henry VIII
C) The anti-begging laws?

13) Was a *diver*?

A) A fisherman
B) One of Queen Elizabeth's attendants who had to dive down to clear any rubbish from her path
C) A little boy who wriggled through holes and windows to steal things?

So the young bacon has picked up a few common con tricks and got a smattering of underworld slang. Maybe he doesn't want to play the part of a coney. Maybe like the young fresh-faced country lad Angel Ben, he fancies becoming a full-fledged rogue himself.

Master Wotton's Training Academy for the Young and Aspiring Nip*, Foist*, Cutpurse* and Shaver*

*Before we enrol at Master Wotton's, you'd better have a quick butchers (butcher's hook, look, get it?) at some more street slang. You don't want to be mistaken for a bacon!

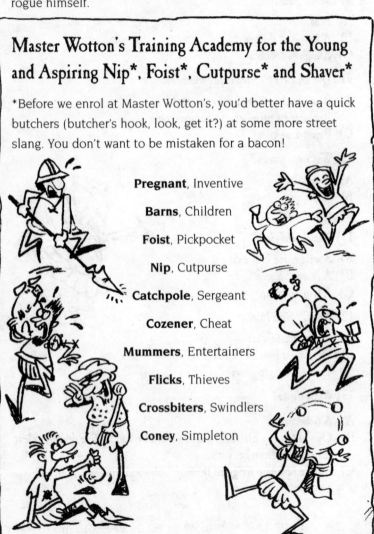

Pregnant, Inventive

Barns, Children

Foist, Pickpocket

Nip, Cutpurse

Catchpole, Sergeant

Cozener, Cheat

Mummers, Entertainers

Flicks, Thieves

Crossbiters, Swindlers

Coney, Simpleton

July 1584.

(SCENE: A den of thieves in Billingsgate, East London. Master Wotton sits at the table in his ruffled shirt and his knee-length blue gown. He has curly hair and a pointed beard and looks like the respectable merchant he once was. In fact Wotton runs a school for thieves. Mottoes are pinned to the wall above the table such as: 'Lift, Shave and Spare not'. 'Lifting' was robbing a shop or house and 'shaving' was stealing a cloak, silver spoon or smallish item.
At Wotton's right hand sits his assistant, known only as Callot Kit. Around the table are ten boys, ranging in age from six to fourteen. Kit is an expert at the black art of the nip and cut, the hook and the foist – i.e., thieving.
The newest recruit is Ben, a country boy nicknamed Angel for his look of blond innocence. Angel is nine, but looks about five. Wotton has high hopes of Angel.)

WOTTON: Come now, let's see if you can earn your beer and meat or are only good for idle bedpressers. Heigh ho, to work, my pregnant barns.

(Hanging from a rope above the table are two thief traps – a pocket full of coins with bells hanging from it and a purse full of silver also decorated with bells. One by one the boys try to remove the dosh from the purse and the pocket without ringing the bells. Ding-a-ling-ding-a-ling go the bells as each boy has a go. There are curses from Wotton and increasingly foul looks from Callot Kit. Then Angel has a go. Moving as quietly as a cat he takes a silver shilling out of the pocket and with a quick flick of his horn thumb has cut the purse without any tinkling bells.
Loud cheers erupt.)

WOTTON: Angel, you're cleverer than you look. You are a public nipper and a most judicial foister.

(All the boys crowd round to congratulate Angel, though he gets some jealous, angry looks. A rare smile crosses Callot Kit's scarred and pock-marked face.)

KIT: Tonight we'll go a-nipping and a-foisting like you've never seen.

WOTTON: Not so fast, Kit. I have Angel in mind for a little job of my own!

(The next day, outside St Paul's Cathedral. A hot summer's day. The walkway outside the cathedral is crowded with booksellers, printers of pamphlets, writers, artists, ladies and gents going for a stroll. There are mummers and lute-players at work and hawkers of sweet treats, pasties and miracle cures. Honest farmers and merchants up from the country on work mix with the city throng. Also at work are the flicks and the crossbiters. Master Wotton and Angel, both finely dressed in cloaks and richly embroidered doublets, are

on the look-out for conies up from the country to crossbite. They spot an honest-looking man in a home-made doublet and Angel drops a coin just near the man's feet. The man spots the coin and, delighted, bends down to pick it up, as does Wotton at the same instant.)

BACON: Oi, that's mine!

WOTTON: And mine too. But come now, my good fellow. Let us see reason. We are both men of the world. What say you we go to a tavern with my servant Angel here and partake of a cup of claret?

(The Bacon is flattered for he takes Wotton and Angel to be city folk of quality. Later, at the Crossed Garter, a pub near St Paul's frequented by gentlemen. Wotton orders a white wine and a claret in silver goblets and toasts his new friend's health.)

WOTTON: *(sipping his drink)* I do declare this wine sorely needs a dash of rosewater and sugar. *(Casually throwing down his cloak, which is old and frayed compared to his fancy doublet, he takes his silver goblet)* I'll rustle up that boy of mine and see if he can add some spice to this cup.

(Wotton disappears outside and his new friend sips his claret happily. After five minutes he starts to wonder where Wotton is. After a quarter of an hour he is very

uneasy. Half an hour later he realizes that he has been cozened. Sure, he has got Wotton's old cloak but he has to pay for the expensive silver goblet.

Later still, at the Red Bull, Bishopsgate. The packed, beery room of a tavern that has been turned into a theatre. Dressed as women, two actors sport on a stage made of planks to admiring roars. Many of the

audience are drunk and not paying attention. Angel gets scarcely a second look as he moves in and out of the crowd. A very drunk man pats him on the head as he passes and a lady says, 'What a pretty barn.' Angel cuts three purses and quietly picks four pockets before a woman notices that her purse has gone. She lets out an angry roar: 'Spades, spades! Nip, nip, call the Catchpole!' There is a commotion as everyone checks their purses and tries to catch the thief.

But it is too late. Angel and Kit have gone. Their takings are nearly two shillings — not bad when a servant would be lucky to make two shillings a month.

Still later still. Dusk is falling. Kit and Angel are walking home on a broad, wealthy road when Kit spots an open window. It is in the gatehouse of a fine mansion. Inside there are clothes fluttering — and no one around to guard them.)

KIT: Hark, Angel. Up there.
(Angel sees the clothes.)

KIT: You be my diver.

ANGEL: I'm afraid, Kit. I don't know how.

KIT: Climb up, lad. I'll keep watch.
(Angel hesitates then agrees with a nod. He wriggles up the wall, finding toeholds in the stone and disappears from sight through the window. Then suddenly Kit hears a roar of pain and a stout head appears at the window — the watchman, after all. Kit doesn't give it a second thought — he scarpers. But Angel is now well and truly in a Tudor pickle, as the watchman takes him by the neck and carts him off to prison.)

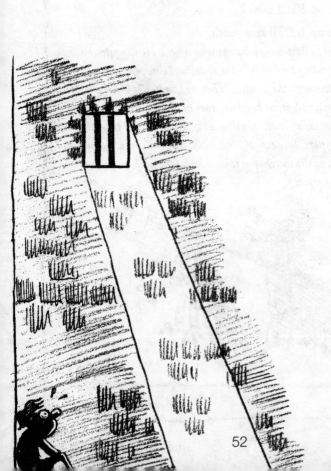

CHAPTER FOUR

𝔓𝔲𝔱𝔯𝔦𝔡 𝔓𝔲𝔫𝔦𝔰𝔥𝔪𝔢𝔫𝔱𝔰

Tudor cops were a bit of a joke. Constables, who were appointed by the parish for a year, were not paid. Very few people wanted the job, but you weren't allowed to refuse. So sometimes constables hired old men to do the job for them.

These feeble granddads with their sticks and dogs weren't exactly feared in criminal circles. Criminals were cleverer and better organized than the Tudor PC plod. The watchmen or bellmen who patrolled the City of London were a bit more effective – but they weren't allowed in the 'liberties', like Southwark. This is why Southwark became a hotbed of gambling dens, theatres and cutpurses.

Tudor cops may have been a laughing stock. But their punishments were no joke. Here's what happened when you were accused of a crime:

The Stocks: You were locked by your feet in a wooden frame while people pelted you with rotten veg.

The Pillory: You were locked by shoulders and arms in a frame with your head sticking out. More rotten veg was thrown at you.

Whipping Post: You were tied to the post and whipped.

Ear Cropping: You could have your ears cut off or your nose slit.

Branding: You could be branded like a cow with the letter F for felon.

Scold's Bridle: Women could be fitted with this horrible metal head-case sometimes with a vicious bit that pierced their tongue just for nagging their husbands.

Ducking Stool: Suspected witches were tied to a stool and ducked in the river, sometimes for minutes at a time. Another test of witchcraft was to throw the witch in the water. If she floated she was a witch and guilty – if she drowned she was innocent (much good it did her!)

Being sent to prison was no better than being branded or whipped. As you might imagine, London's prisons, such as Newgate, the Counter and the Clink, were smelly, overcrowded and unbearably rotten. If the executioner didn't get you diseases might well do the job first. There were thousands and thousands of people wasting away in London's prisons who had done nothing wrong.

You could get sent to prison in Tudor times for:

> not being able to pay your debts
>
> for questioning the right of King Henry to be the English pope
>
> for being out of your home parish without permission
>
> because someone accuses you of wrongdoing
>
> on suspicion of being a witch
>
> for questioning Queen Liz's possible marriage to a Frenchman (one man had his hand cut off for this crime)
>
> for stealing two sheets (one woman was hanged for this crime)

The gaolers were a greedy lot who extracted 'garnish' or bribes for everything – unlocking the gate, food, water, even taking their chains off. They brewed beer and sold it to the prisoners. If you could pay for the poshest cells or Master Side you could live decently, with good food and wine. You could even leave the prison for 20p a day.

If you had no money you ended up in a dungeon called The Hole. There you lived – huddled forty to a tiny room – on charity. You had to share baskets full of scraps of food that might have been mauled by dogs and spat out by children.

ANGEL'S ADVENTURES IN THE COUNTER

(Shafts of sunlight from the barred window pierces the gloom of the prison cell, which is in Wood Street. Angel Ben is lying on the floor,

other prisoners are chained to the wall or have their hands held together by thumbscrews. They lie so close together on the filthy floor that you could be forgiven for thinking you are in a graveyard, littered with moving corpses. One man lies in the corner groaning. He is dying of the sweating sickness. A

child weeps over its dying father. The stench of excrement from the jake or loo in the corner – which has not been emptied for several days – is overpowering. Horn-Thumb Hal, a burly thief in velvet bodkin, is teasing Angel.)

HORN-THUMB HAL:	You're for it, Ben. You shall dance the hempen jig * afore dusk.
BEN:	You shall ride up Holborn Hill* afore I do, Hal. Why, you foisted a gentleman's purse with three gold sovereigns.
	(Hal laughs. It is a horrible, sinister sound.)
HAL:	Me? I have friends, lad, friends in high places. I'll be sipping wine in Master's Side* afore the day is out. Then I'll disappear. No more time in the Hole* for me.
	(The warder waddles in. He has two stomachs and four chins and is wearing a fine gold chain. He slimes up to Hal with a smile.)

WARDER: Any garnish for me, fine gentlemen? They are having venison today at Master's Side.

HAL: Has Angler Abe brought the sovereign?

WARDER: No, fine master.

HAL: The flap-mouth knave! He has crossed me!

(Suddenly the warder is not so greasy. Without wasting another word he kicks Hal into the corner and beckons to Angel.)

WARDER: You! Boy! Get thee here. A gentleman has paid for your release. You're going to school!

*To dance the hempen jig and ride up Holborn Hill both mean to be hanged. The Master's Side was the posh part of the prison and the Hole, yep you guessed, it really was a hole

Torture was more common during Tudor times than ever before or since in London. It was only used in cases of treason as it was outlawed in the common law. Thankfully torture was finally made illegal in 1640.

Ye Olde Tudor Torturer's Handbook

Or

The Gentle Art of Jack Spratt, King Henry's Torturer-in-Chief

I have been a torturer for many, many years now. I'm writing this down so that youngsters entering the ~~profession~~ job will learn it without the many years of trial wot I had.

A torturer has to be of a gentle and godly sort. This is by His Majesty King Henry VIII's will. There are to be no roughhousing, I don't beat and bloody the prisoners for fun. Torture has to be done right and it is only for those traitors wot have gone against the king.

The pains should begin if words have not led the prisoner to confess. Then the prisoner should be shown the torture chamber and the fings I keep there. If he still does not confess then by and by it should go on to bloodier things till the prisoner is afeared for his life and begging for mercy.

Remember there is no room for soft feelings for those who have gone against God and the king's laws.

I find that once prisoners are thrown in the Hole in the Tower of London they soon soften up nicely - fearing for their health, no doubt, what with the rats and the damp and dripping water and screams in the night. It lets their ~~imagineetio~~ fears go a bit bonkers.

After that you could try a nice spot of 'tormento de

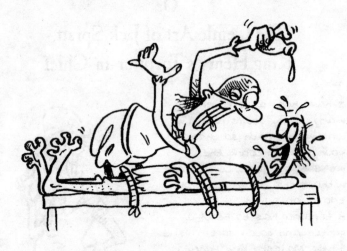

toca'. This is when water is poured drop by drop on to the prisoner's bare skin, while he is strapped down. This drives people nuts and for the weaker sort of men and wimmin should give you your confession.

For more manly sorts I find those little helpers that break bones and stuff are really good. I've got a brand new machine that breaks your teeth - I used it on Thomas Culpepper, who was accused of having relations with Catherine Howard, the king's fifth wife (a strumpet) that did horribly betray him along with other men. The king was so pleased with me after that confession I got five gold sovereigns from His most generous Majesty plus all the bees I could eat from the royal table.

Other things that break bones are the bootes for feet, the thumbscrews for thumbs, and pilliwinks for breaking fingers one by one.

If your prisoner is an ~~obstinat~~ tough sort of rascal you may need to used somefink a little bit stronger (I find them catholics and religious prisoners very wrong-minded). An iron collar, for example, can be screwed round their neck, till they stop breathing.

Wimmin, as you know, are easy to break. But I've had one old hag, her name was Anne Askew, wot was really tough. She really insulted the king and he was very angry with her. (I fink she was too catholic for his liking.) We had to tie her down and stretch her on the rack until her bones popped out. This wasn't easy.

She still didn't confess. She was probably a witch and anyway was taken to Smithfield to be burned.

My boys (torture is a manly job but it ain't always easy) are weights what are loaded onto the prisoner till he is pressed to death. I call them my Ace of Spades and they are also known as peine forte et dure – that's french for painful! Nah only kidding, it means 'strong and hard'. I only use them if all the other tortures have failed. And it ain't much good then cos the prisoner will probably be quite dead.

That's why I always say to the young lads. 'Lads,' I say, 'If you've got to go in for peine forte et dure it means you ain't explored every avenue, painwise.'

CHAPTER FIVE

𝔖𝔦𝔠𝔨𝔢𝔫𝔦𝔫𝔤 𝔖𝔠𝔥𝔬𝔬𝔩𝔰

If you think your school is bad you should try time-travelling back to a Tudor school. London schools like St Paul's and Westminster were really, really rotten.

Here are just five reasons why you wouldn't like going to a Tudor school. And, believe me, there are more.

1. School starts at 5 a.m. (yes, in the morning!). This is before the sun has even risen. Sleepyheads are awakened with a thwack of the cane.

2. School goes on and on till 5 p.m., with only short breaks for meals and play.

3. You are expected to read and write and speak Latin before you go to school at the age of six or seven. That is a lot of studying when you are not much more than a toddler.

4. A beating is the punishment for every offence – no matter how minor. One schoolmaster priest whipped a boy till he fainted, then admitted he 'has done nothing to deserve all this, but it is necessary to curb his spirit by wholesome discipline'.

5. You are expected to take your hat off and address your master on bended knee. You must never speak unless spoken to. Exceptions are made for emergencies. You might, for example, be allowed to say, 'Excuse me, Master, the school is on fire.'

Sounds gruesome, doesn't it? No wonder the scholar Erasmus, who was against too much beating, compared schools to 'torture chambers' and wrote: 'Blows and shouts, sobs and howls fill the air. Then it is wondered that the growing boy hates learning.'

The children of royals and nobility had it easier, they were taught at home by tutors. Poorer children didn't go to school at all, but from an early age helped their mum or dad with their work. Later on they became apprentice butchers or ironmongers. But for the sons of such folk as merchants and physicians, and some cleverer poor boys who got free education, school was their horrible lot.

Skool Rules O.K.

Here are the rules of Westminster School, near the Thames:

> NO LAUGHING, TALKING, GIGGLING OR SMIRKING IF
> SOMEONE READS POORLY
>
> NO SCUFFLING AND DON'T ANSWER BACK IF ASKED TO
> DO SOMETHING
>
> WHOMSOEVER REPLIES IN ENGLISH TO A QUESTION IN
> LATIN GETS A STROKE (BEATING)
>
> IF DICE ARE FOUND IN ANYONE'S HAND LET HIM GET A
> BLOW FROM A BIRCH ON NAKED FLESH.
>
> (NO PRIZES FOR GUESSING WHAT THE PUNISHMENT WAS
> IF YOU BROKE ANY RULE. YEP, THAT'S RIGHT, A BEATING.)

But there is one reason you might like a Tudor School. Rack your brains. Is it?

A) Because schoolchildren had longer holidays

B) Schoolchildren had good homemade food with lots of puddings – unlike today's rotten school meals

C) Schoolchildren didn't have spelling tests

Answer: C. Truth is, they had very short holidays and the food was pretty rotten. But there were no spelling tests. You could write words like they sounded ('phonetically') and if everyone wrote differently no one cared. So you could write school, scol, schole, scool, scole or anything you liked. As long as it sounded about right – and you wouldn't get marked down.

Here is what a school day at Westminster would have been like.

The Diary of Angel Ben aged 5 and 3/4

January 30 1589

There is somefink worse than prisson. It is called skool. After prisson I thot life cant get wurse. It can.

The marster awoked me from bed at five o clock. He is shawt wiv no hare on his hed and very ugly. He called out and struk me wiv the wip for bean slow. We prade in Latin and then washt. The worter wos freezin. Then at 8 for too ours we stood rand the marster and chanted Latin.

Then we had manchet, that's a sweet bred, for brekfust. The ale was good and strong.

At nine mor scool. Boring Greek.

In braik I wos playin with my frend Tom at cudgels. We fand sticks for cudgels. We wos playing good. I beat Tom on the hed and he beet me. Then the marster came and stopt us.

We were beeted very badly. I fainted though I swor to God I will not let a word pass my lips. My bottom is now a bloddy mes.

Still huzzah huzzah, scool's over for today!

So all in all school was something the smart Tudor child would bunk off at all costs. No wonder London's children used to sing:

I wish my master were a hare
And his book hounds were
And I myself a jolly hunter
To blow my horn I would not spare
For if he were dead I would not care!

CHAPTER SICKS (SIX)
𝔉𝔬𝔲𝔩 𝔉𝔬𝔬𝔡

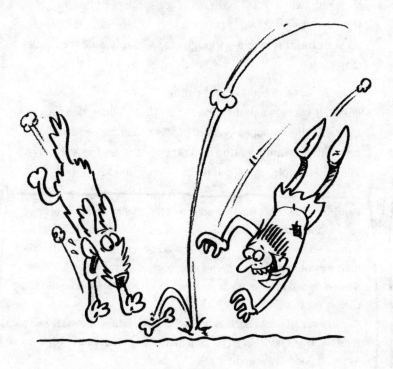

Tudor Londoners, from commoners to kings, loved nothing more than a good hog. If you don't believe me take a look at a picture of King Henry VIII in later life – now there's a man who loved his feed!

In the leaner years poorer Londoners lived on air and turnips. But richer Tudors weren't bothered, they ate like porkers. A meal could last from 11 a.m. to 7 p.m. and be interrupted only by frequent trips to the chamber pot!

And boy did they drink. Ale was drunk like water, which was probably a good thing because London water was rank and full of foul floating things. Everyone, even babies and kids, liked their pint, which must have made for some pretty drunken toddlers. It would take a pretty tough 21st-century kid to keep up with Tudor drinking – though ale was fairly watery by today's standards.

But food wasn't just about eating. Not for the lords and ladies. It was also about showing off (mainly how rich they were). At their palaces every dish was accompanied by a lot of fuss, with servants waiting upon them hand and foot. Henry VIII, for example, in his palace at Whitehall had:

Pantlers to taste his food for poison in the kitchen. Pantlers also carved stale loaves of bread into 'trenchers', that is little boats which were filled up with meat. The stale bread trenchers, which had soaked up the meat juices, were given to the poor.

Sewers tasted his food for poison in the dining room before the carvers got to work.

Carvers cut off the head, legs and other nasty bits of the meat and put it on the king's trencher so he didn't have to get his hands dirty by fishing around in the common pot for meat.

Cup bearers tasted his wine for poison and held a cover under his cup to catch any slobbery drips.

Sewers and carvers to King Henry VIII were thought to be posh jobs which were filled by earls and lords, who served the king on bended knee. Even young King Eddie had grown men falling to their knees as they served him his nosh.

And God, could the nosh go on and on. Here is a sample of the kind of meal that Young King Ed would have sat down to at Whitehall or Liz would have enjoyed at Richmond Palace:

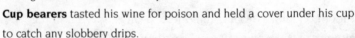

FIRST COURSE

Mini pasties filled with cod

Meat in cinnamon sauce

Beef marrow

Fritters

Eels in spicy puree

Loach in cold green sauce

Saltwater fish

Cuts of roast meat

SECOND COURSE

Frumenty
(wheat boiled in milk with sugar and spices)

Freshwater fish

Broth with bacon

Capon pasties

Bream and eel pasties

Blancmange

Tarts

Jelly

Cakes

Leche lumbarde (a sort of flavoured custard)

THIRD COURSE

Spiced wine (for digestion)

Wafers

Fruit

Nuts and raisins

Cheese

The Tudors may have been very, very greedy but they were very strict about table manners. Which of the following were considered bad table manners in Tudor times?

1) Scratching your bottom at table

2) Belching after your meal

3) Using a knife and fork

4) Picking your nose and dropping it into your food

5) Blowing your nose with your fingers.

6) Dropping your bones on the floor after your meal.

7) Eating all the food on your plate.

Answers:

1) Bad.

2) Good.

3) Bad in some circles, such as the navy where they were considered unmanly. Scooping food out of the common trenchers with your hands and eating with your hands was good manners. Spoons were used for soup, but cutlery didn't come into fashion till much later.

4) Bad.

5) Bad.

6) Good manners in aristocrat homes.

7) Bad manners for toffs.

Here are some useful tips about good table manners from a book published in 1557:

Your mouth not too full when you eat;

Don't smack your lips as do hogs

Don't gnaw the bones as do dogs;

Don't pick your teeth at the table sitting,

Don't do on your meat too much spitting.

Revolting Re

Smelly Sausages

In Tudor times there were no preservatives so they ̶ ̶ ̶
with clever ways of making rank, stinky meat less yu̶ ̶
following recipe for sausages. (But don't blame me if yo̶
terrible tummyache!)

Take the meat from an old boar and chop it very finely

Mix the meat with a handful of sage and season with ginger and
pepper

Put mixture in a great sheep's gut

Let it lie three nights in brine

Boil it

Hang it up in a chimney where fire is usually kept

Move house (only kidding)

These sausages will keep for a whole year. Enjoy!

Hot Hedgehogs

Ingredients

2lbs minced pork
2 tablespoons breadcrumbs
1/2 teaspoon ginger
1/2 tsp mace
2 tsps salt
1/4 tsp pepper
2 tbsps of sugar
1 tbsp soft butter
4 tbsps vegetable stock
2 ounces slivered almonds
green/brown colouring
egg

, breadcrumbs, spices and butter with the beaten egg ...m a ball. Place in a buttered pan and cook, covered for one hour. Baste the ball regularly with the butter melted in the vegetable stock. Stick the slivered almonds – which you dye with the colouring – all over the pudding so that they look like the quills of a hedgehog.

This recipe is an example of the Tudor love of practical jokes. Illusion foods were meant to trick the diner as much as to appeal to their taste buds.

One cookery book describes how to make animals out of wood or plaster which you covered with marzipan. Then you covered the marzipan with cinnamon and sugar breadcrumbs so they looked like roasted and breaded fowl! Oooo the giggles and fun when your guests bit into marzipan and plaster and lost all their teeth!

One of the most famous Tudor fantasy foods was blackbird pie. This was a proper pie which you filled with blackbirds or finches… or if you were feeling particularly naughty, live frogs to make the ladies shriek! This pie is remembered in the nursery rhyme:

Sing a song o'sixpence, a pocket full of rye
Four and twenty blackbirds baked in a pie
When the pie was opened
The birds began to sing
Wasn't that a tasty dish to set before the king

CHAPTER SEVEN

I'd Rather Eat Toenails

Or The Tudor Guide to Visiting the Doctors

(4.30 a.m. The dawn light is breaking through the holes in the walls of a rough dwelling in Stinking Lane in the crowded slums of Cheapside. Will Bayley, costermonger and father of too many children to count, lies on a rough wooden pallet, which is softened by a straw mattress. He is sweating, his eyes burn with fever and he mutters wildly. His baby daughter, Peg, in her swaddling clothes, hangs from her peg on the wall. She would be bawling but her mouth is gagged. His other children are bundled in bed next to him. His wife Anne, who is already up at her chores, waddles into the bedroom.)

ANNE: Will. Shame on thee. You must up and go to East Cheap market else you will miss the day's work and the barns will have no bread and beer this day.

(Will moans.)

ANNE: Will, up I say. And you lazy bedpressers too. *(She shakes the children up out of bed and they stumble out hastily. Will mutters some more. The word Jesu' and Hallelujah can be heard. Anne approaches the bed and when she sees how red and sweaty William is, she lets out a shrill scream of fright.)*

ANNE: You are sick. Oooooooh!. What is to become of us, poor fatherless orphans. Where will we end up! Bedlam, I suppose. We must hurry to the sawbones.'

(At the mention of sawbones – the doctors – William sits bolt upright in bed, his eyes pop and he screams too. The children have joined in the screams, so it's hard to hear what he is saying above the racket.)

WILL: I'd rather eat my own toenails. I'd rather rip my own arms off!

(Later, at the House of Doc Septimus Frogget of Cudgel Alley, off Bread Lane. William nearly collapses when he sees Doc Frogget's red and white striped barber's pole. The pole represents the bloody bandages surgeons hang out to dry. Inside on the table lie his instruments: a saw, pliers, scissors, sharp knives, wrenches. They look more like something a plumber would use than a doctor. In fact Doc Frogget would be better at fixing people's toilets, 'if they had any', than curing them. Doc Frogget, in a gore-spattered smock, is pouring boiling oil on the bloody stump where a man's ear used to be. The ear lies on the table. The man is a tramp whose punishment was to have his ear cut off. The tramp is drunk and raving with pain. Loud knocking is heard.)

DOC F: Come in, come in, What is it? Can't you see I'm busy?

ANNE: *(her eyes red from weeping)* My husband is dying.

DOC F: *(looking Will up and down)* A poor sort of lad but I can cure him. It will cost a sovereign.

(Will moans and Anne starts to cry.)

ANNE: Have mercy. Will only makes three sovereigns a year. We have eight barns. They'll starve.

DOC F: Hmm. Eight shillings. My final offer.

(*Anne silently pours out a small pile of silver pennies on the table. The family's life savings. Frogget mutters crossly but after shoving the screaming tramp on a bed in the corner, undresses Will and examines him.*)

DOC F: Where is his piss?

(*Anne produces a small bottle filled with Will's urine. Frogget takes it, holds it to the light.*)

DOC F: It is not the plague. I see no buboes [horrible sores]. This man is a weakly thing. He must eat eggs and avoid anything that over-stimulates his eyes like garlic, peppers, bright sunshine or wind. His blood is slow and he has the sweat. I must bleed him.

(*Will has almost fainted but Doc Frogget carries on anyway. He carries him to his operating table and ties him down. Then he forces alcohol down his throat. He cuts open Will's vein and blood comes pouring out into a small cup. Two days later Will is sicker than ever, his red feverishness has been replaced by a white deathly pallor. As a last resort Anne has decided to take him to see Dr Simon Foreman, the noted magician at his house in Lambeth, south of London. Foreman – who later will successfully predict the hour and manner of his own death – invokes spirits, tells fortunes and also heals the sick. Though he treats nobles and gentlemen he often treats poorer clients free. Foreman's study is full of big books and charts with strange astrological markings. He gazes into a crystal ball, then gives Anne his advice.*)

FOREMAN: You must give him this potion and keep him warm but not hot. Make sure he takes plenty of beer. He will get better in ten days' time.

(Anne, weeping, offers Foreman some clothes – all she has left. Foreman waves the clothes away and sits in front of his crystal. Intently he peers into it for a few seconds.)

FOREMAN: You will pay me in two years' time.

(Foreman rises from the table and stretches out his hands in farewell. Ten days later William Bayley is better and back at his stall in Cheapside. Hale and hearty he bellows out his wares.)

WILLIAM: Jellied eels, mussels, cockles, fresh pike. Roll up, roll up the finest eels in fair Queen Bess's land!

Help Me Doc, I'm as Sick as a Tudor Parrot

Medicine might have been a bit of a joke. But would you get into Tudor medical college? See if you can pass this test.

1. A man comes to see you with a bad haircut. Do you?
A) Send him away. You're a doctor, for God's sake, not a hairdresser. You didn't waste all those years in medical college to be a barber.
B) Charge him a penny and cut his hair.
C) Call the police.

2. A ten-year-old girl comes to you with obvious signs of the plague. She could easily be dead within hours. Do you?
A) Make a run for it to the countryside. Plague is really catching and you don't want to get it.
B) Squeeze her purplish-black boils, called buboes, till they burst.
C) Tell her not to eat lettuce.

3. A woman is brought to you with the sweating sickness. The symptoms are a high fever and it is so feared that it caused Henry VII to delay his coronation. Do you?
A) Put a headless pigeon on her lower parts to drain out the bad 'gases'.
B) Tell her to eat plenty of lettuce.
C) Wrap her in a swaddling sheet and hang her from a peg in the wall like a baby.

4. A small boy has the 'new' disease smallpox. Do you?
A) Give him some aspirin.
B) Hang a red cloth over his window.
C) Make sure he takes plenty of caster oil in vinegar.

5. A wealthy landowner is brought to you with scrofula, a kind of tuberculosis that causes scroggy ulcers at the neck. Do you?

A) Plead with Queen Elizabeth to heal him with her magic touch.

B) Tell him to go horse-riding – fresh air cures scrofula.

C) Mix turpentine, radishes, chicken droppings, almonds and urine and tell him to drink the mixture thrice daily?

6. You are a doctor called in to see King Henry VIII and realize he is on his deathbed. Do you?

A) Give him some arsenic to kill him.

B) Keep quiet about how ill he is.

C) Tell him to call a priest, he is dying.

1 – B. Doctors often doubled as barbers and were known as barber-surgeons.

2 – C. They didn't have a clue that plague was spread by rats.

3 – A. Don't ask.

4 – B. This is one of the few Tudor cures that works. It was later found that sun rays causes pox scarring and a red cloth or paper over the window can cut this out!

5 – A. It was believed that royal personages could cure scrofula by their touch – it was called 'the king's evil'. All the Tudors went round touching hundreds of people. History doesn't tell us how many they cured though!

6 – B. King Henry made it a treasonable offence to foretell his death. So when he was dying his doctors were too scared to tell him. Only Sir Anthony Denny, one of his close friends, was prepared to risk it, telling him to prepare for death.

CHAPTER EIGHT

Fierce Fun

How would you like to be a Tudor Londoner? You'd probably run a mile in hobnailed boots rather than travel back to those stinky times. But life in London circa 1550 wasn't all turnips and torture.

There was also fun!

Tudor Londoners, from labourers to kings, liked nothing better than having fun. They played cards, backgammon, bowls, danced, listened to music, invented silly riddles or went to the bear- and bull-baiting rings in Southwark or had a day out watching the hangman at work at the gallows at Tyburn Tree near present-day Marble Arch. King Henry loved games and sports of all types. He had new covered tennis courts built at his palaces in Whitehall and Hampton Court (where you can still see them). And he loved hunting, jousting and archery.

In the courts of King Henry and Liz there was never an excuse needed for a party – for dancing and dressing up, with mummers and lute players and all sorts of fancy dress.

And then, for rich and poor alike, there was always the theatre, which showed plays by the likes of Marlowe and Shakespeare. Actors were regarded by the Tudors as little better than vagabonds. They could have their ears cut off like any old clapperdudgeon if they weren't protected by a nobleman. The first nobleman to allow his actors to perform to the general public was the Earl of Leicester. His actors staged their first play in the courtyard of the Bull Inn in Bishopsgate in

1574. Plays soon caught on and there was an explosion of theatre building. James Burbage, an actor and manager of Leicester's actors, built the first London theatre in Holywell Lane in Finsbury Fields in 1577. Shakespeare's plays, like those of his pal Christopher Marlowe, were performed in open-air theatres like the Globe, which was built on the banks of the river Thames in the 1590s. Other famous London theatres were the Swan in the Paris Gardens and the Rose – all close to each other in Southwark.

In Tudor times women were banned from being actresses so all the women's parts were played by young lads. Maybe that's why so many of Will's heroines dress up as boys! Will's plays can seem like Tudor torture now. But in his own day people watched them for hot news. They were better than the newspapers. (Which didn't exist as we know them now – so rumour and gossip did the job instead – not too different from some of our own beloved newspapers if you think about it.) In fact old Will got so tangled up in politics he was lucky that Queen Bess didn't use one of her favourite punishments on him and make him 'shorter by a head.'

This is how it happened:

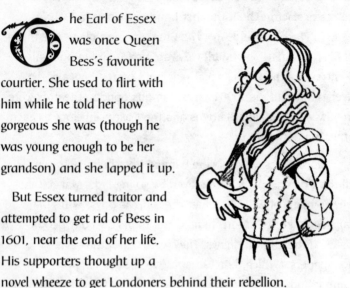

The Earl of Essex was once Queen Bess's favourite courtier. She used to flirt with him while he told her how gorgeous she was (though he was young enough to be her grandson) and she lapped it up.

But Essex turned traitor and attempted to get rid of Bess in 1601, near the end of her life. His supporters thought up a novel wheeze to get Londoners behind their rebellion.

They paid actors to stage the full version of Shakespeare's play *Richard* II. Richard II had been made to abdicate about two hundred years earlier, to make way for Henry Bolingbroke' and the people of London were instrumental in letting Henry into the city to take the crown. The abdication scene of the play was usually omitted because it seemed to touch a raw nerve with Elizabeth. So for a Tudor audience the parallels between Bess and Richard weren't hard to spot. The plotters had people going around muttering that Bess was as bad, not to mention as drippy, as Richard. Luckily for lovers of literature (all right, you may not be among them) when Essex's rebellion was put down and the Earl was sentenced to death, the Stratford bard was spared.

Londoners loved insults and Shakespeare had some of the best. Try these out on the next person who insults you and watch them turn purple!

You're unfit for any place but hell
You're as rheumatic as two dry toasts
Sell your face for five-pence and it's dear
You poisonous bunch-backed toad
You are a very ragged wort
You burly-boned beef-witted flap-dragon
You map of woe

In fact good old Queen Elizabeth actually banned plays on Thursdays because she thought they were frivolous amusements that were distracting people from the good, manly pleasures of bear-baiting and bull-fighting. Bears still roamed wild in English forests and everyone from commoners to kings loved the sport. Even as a little girl Liz had kept bears for this sport. At a bear-baiting the poor animal was chained to a post while a pack of crazed dogs were set on it.

The bear valiantly tried to fight the dogs off with its giant paws. Bears that outlived loads of dogs became famous (and even loved.) They were given pet names like Harry Hunks and Sacherson.

Liz absolutely adored the sport. When she visited Kenilworth in 1575 a grand bear-baiting was arranged with fifteen dogs set on the bear to tear its throat out. 'It was very pleasant,' wrote the courtier Robert Laneham, who was part of the royal party, to watch the bear 'with biting, with clawing … with blood and slaver' trying to get save its life.

In 1598 a German traveller Paul Hentzner went to a public bear-baiting in the Bear Gardens in Southwark. People sat in circles, watching the fun while sellers of nuts and fruit hawked their wares. Almost everyone smoked tobacco in clay pipes. After the crowd had enjoyed a bear being tortured by dogs they lapped up another sport. A bear was fastened to a post and six men stood around it with whips. Hentzner thought it fun to watch the bear breaking the whips and trying to defend itself. Sometimes bear-baiting ended with the torment of a pony – a monkey was tied to a pony's back and dogs bit the pony's legs while it tried to shake off both the dogs and the monkey!

As you can see, the Tudors' idea of animal rights was non-existent. But their idea of football was just as terrible. In fact a Tudor match would cause a premiership referee to have a fit and there wouldn't be enough red cards in the world to go round.

MATCH OF YE DAYE

Today's Top Match:
Watling Street Wonders v Cheapside Utd.

Our Premiership Correspondent Gary Spinniker, joins us
live from the football pitch at Smithfield.

Thanks Des, footie fans will
know that this semi-final of the
Henry VIII trophy has been
eagerly awaited, with the
outsiders Cheapside Utd heavily
fancied after their awesome
demolition of favourites Watling
Street Wonders.

United's rising star David
Peckham's trademark blond quiff
flashed everywhere on the field.

He took the ball early on with a superb tackle of Michael Owers
and kept the ball despite having his shin smashed with a flying
lunge, his ankle twisted and his nose broken.

Only when his eye was blacked by Gary Gobbin's fist did 'Pecs'
give up the ball. Later he wowed fans by a revenge attack on the
thuggish Gobbins, who was stretchered off the field with a
broken back. His final goal, a superb free kick from a good 200
yards led to a good-natured pitch invasion.

Final score Cheapside 22 Wonders 18.

Moaning minnies have been complaining that rules must be introduced into football to stamp out 'unnecessary' deaths on the field. But after this good-natured match local surgeons reported just one fatality – and that was only of a member of the crowd. Only fifteen players were injured, three broken noses, a broken back and ten twisted ankles. Friendly matches like this prove that regulation of the game is not needed! That's all from me, Gary Spinniker, now it's back to the studio.

Tudor football was savage. The object of the game was to put the ball through the opponents' goal, which could be as much as two or three miles away. There were no other rules! Football was banned by a statute in Edward II's reign in 1314 but was still played. Philip Stubbs, a Protestant, was one of the many people appalled by the broken necks and noses running with blood: 'There are no rules that I can tell,' he wrote in 1583. 'The man with the ball must run with it for his life.'

Tudor Riddles

They may have lived deep in the rotten, old past and their football may have made the premiership look like a village tea party but in some ways the Tudors were pretty smart. If you don't believe me, try some of their riddles. The first one comes from Will Shakespeare's Hamlet

Q: Who builds stronger than either the mason, the shipwright or the carpenter?

A: The gallows-maker, for that outlives a thousand tenants.

Q: A vessel I have
That is round like a pear
Moist in the middle
And surrounded with hair
And often it happens
That water flows there

A: An eye.

Q: Which came first, the chicken or the egg?

A: There is no answer to this one. Though the Tudors claimed
it was the chicken 'when God made her'.

The strangest Tudor sport was executions. Many hundreds of people went to see hangings and they got dressed up in their finest clothes for the event. At London's most famous gallows, called Tyburn Tree in present-day Marble Arch, there was even seating for spectators. Sellers of sweets and pies would circle among the excited crowd as the hanging took place – it was quite a party atmosphere.

The prisoner would march in procession from Newgate for the plebs and from the Tower for the gentry and hundreds would cheer or boo them on the way. They would stop at the St George and Blue Boar for a 'parting cup' of sherry while the common prisoners would have a bowl of ale at St Giles-in-the-Fields. Often prisoners would arrive to be hanged dead drunk. The crowd at 'the fatal tree' would really expect something special in the way of a 'death speech'.

You can imagine the nervous prisoner reading out his death speech. Even more nerve-shredding than appearing in a school play. Prisoners would be judged as to have 'died well' or 'died badly' (not that they'd be around to read the reviews of their performances). Their speeches were printed up in pamphlets and pored over by all sorts of people.

You see the Tudors could turn even death into a good show! And as we've learnt they had the most brilliant playwrights, bloody and brutal kings and queens, terrible diseases and foul food in our history. Luckily London has changed a lot since then. Most of Tudor London is, thankfully, long gone but read on to discover places you can visit to catch a glimpse of life in those horrid times.

Places To Go and Things To Do

Most of Tudor London has disappeared – but if you look hard you can still find some gems which have survived the centuries.

The George Inn, 77 Borough High Street, Southwark, SE1 1NH is the oldest inn in London with an original gallery, like the one which Tudors would have used to watch the plays of Shakespeare.

Sutton House, 2 and 4 Homerton High Street, Hackney, E9 6JQ was built in 1535 – when Hackney was still a tiny village – by Ralph Sutton, one of Henry VIII courtiers. An exhibition tells the story of the house and its owners – from the Tudors to Victorian schoolmistresses. www.nationaltrust.org.uk. Tel 020 8986 2264.

The original Globe theatre was destroyed in 1613, when an ember from a cannon used in one of Shakespeare's plays set light to the thatched roof. **Shakespeare's Globe**, New Globe Walk, Bankside, SE1 9DT, is a brilliant replica that celebrates the Bard's life and work. It features plays and an exhibition on Elizabethan theatre. www.shakespeares-globe.org. Tel 020 7902 1500.

The British Museum, Great Russell Street, Bloomsbury, WC1B 3DG, is a fantastic museum that has something for everyone. Treasures from Tudor times include Queen Elizabeth's glass jug, the warrant for the execution of Mary Queen of Scot's and Shakespeare's signed will. It also holds the looking glass of Elizabethan magician Dr John Dee.
www.thebritishmuseum.ac.uk. Tel 020 7637 7384.

Goldsmiths' Hall, Foster Lane, EC2V 6BN. is the hall of one of the biggest tradesman's guilds. It dates back to before Tudor times but the Goldsmiths' are the proud owners of a golden cup that Queen Elizabeth I is said to have drunk from at her coronation.

Canonbury Tower, Canonbury Place, Islington, N1 2NQ, is a rare survival from Tudor times. It was the home of one of Queen Elizabeth's richest subjects Sir John Spencer.
www.canonbury.ac.uk. Tel 020 7226 6256.

The Tower of London, Tower Hill, EC3N 4AB, was where some of London's grisliest tortures and most foul beheadings took place here. The guards, nicknamed Beefeaters, do great tours. Who knows, if you're unlucky you might even bump into Anne Boleyn's ghost. www.hrp.org.uk. Tel 020 7709 0765.

Queen Elizabeth I lies buried at **Westminster Abbey**, Westminster, SW1P 3PA, in a splendid chapel built by her grandfather. Her sister Mary and cousin Mary Queen of Scots are also buried here. There is also a monument to Shakespeare here. www.westminster-abbey.org. Tel 020 7222 5152.

Hampton Court Palace, East Moseley, Surrey, KT8 9AU, was built by Cardinal Wolsey who gave it to his master King Henry VIII – to try and suck up to him. It didn't work and Wolsey just beat the executioner's axe by dying of natural causes. The royal tennis courts and the fantastic Tudor kitchens with their great ovens and roasting spits are worth a visit. www. hrp.org.uk. Tel 020 8781 9500.

Bruce Castle, Lordship Lane, N17, is an amazing castle in the North London suburb of Tottenham. Well worth a visit although it's a bizarre Tudor egg onto which a later Georgian shell has been added. www.hanringey.gov.uk. Tel 020 8808 8772.

The Old Operating Theatre, Museum and Herb Garrett, 9a St Thomas St, London SE1 9RY, gives an insight into grisly Tudor medicine and you can see the interesting herbs and knives doctors used when they were more like butchers! There are lots of special events here. www.thegarret.org.uk. Tel 020 7955 4791.

The London Dungeon, 28–34 Tooley Street, London Bridge, SE1 2SZ, is London's top spot for terrifying tortures and disgusting dungeons. Not for the faint-hearted but fierce fun. www.thedungeons.com. Tel 020 7403 7221.

The Clink Prison Museum, 1 Clink Street, London SE1 9DG, offers more fantastic dungeons and instruments of torture. Imagine life as someone who really got in the way of horrible Henry VIII! www.clink.co.uk. Tel 020 7382 1558.

OTHER BOOKS FROM WATLING STREET YOU'LL LOVE

IN THIS SERIES:

The Timetraveller's Guide to Roman London
by Olivia Goodrich
Find out just why Rome's craziest emperors invaded cool, cruel
Britannia and built a city besides the Thames.
ISBN 1-904153-06-2

•

The Timetraveller's Guide to Saxon and Viking London
by Joshua Doder
Journey back to London when it was home to some of the
funniest names and the foulest food in English history!
ISBN 1-904153-07-0

•

The Timetraveller's Guide to Medieval London
by Christine Kidney
Scratch, sniff and itch your way around the capital during its
smelliest period in history.
ISBN 1-904153-08-9

•

The Timetraveller's Guide to Shakespeare's London
by Joshua Doder
William Shakespeare is our greatest writer; read all about him,
his plays and the big bad city he lived and worked in.
ISBN 1-904153-10-0

•

The Timetraveller's Guide to Victorian London
by Natasha Narayan
Get robbed and meet the snobs on a tour of Queen Vic's
top town.
ISBN 1-904153-11-9

In case you have difficulty finding any Watling St books in your local bookshop, you can place orders directly through

BOOKPOST
Freepost
PO Box 29
Douglas
Isle of Man IM99 1BQ

Telephone 01634 836000
email: bookshop@enterprise.net